Dinnington Days Gone By

INTRODUCTION

This is a selection of photographs collected over many years by Dinnington & District History Society, lead by Roy Newman and Pam Cook.

All members of the Society have worked diligently to produce this unique collection. Local people have also been generous in loaning their photographs.

The book shows Dinnington and the surrounding villages from their beginnings as a farming community until the latter part of the 1900s.

The History Society has also filmed local personalities many of whom are now deceased. Their fascinating personal experiences have been captured for posterity.

We hope you enjoy our book and would like to thank Arc Publishing and Print for making these images available to a wider public.

Index

Published by Arc Publishing and Print
166 Knowle Lane
Sheffield
S11 9SJ

Telephone 07809 172872

OLD FALCON INN. 1900. B Adams Proprietor. The Inn can be seen to the right with the living quarters on the left.

THE SECOND FALCON HOTEL. 1930-36. This replaced the preceding Inn and was a social port of call for the top of the village. It was situated across from the Church in Falcon Square.
The square takes it name from the hotel.

Old view of Laughton Road, Dinnington. c1900

Laughton High Street. A Hive of Activity.

DINNINGTON COLLIERY WORKERS. All in their 'uniform' of flat caps. Two hold their water bottles which often contained cold tea. These men were the salt of the earth and helped make Dinnington the place it is today.

Dinnington Church c1905

The Church is shown before its extension

FALCON SQUARE AND CHURCH DINNINGTON. Shown in the foreground of the picture is the bus shelter, which had two separate compartments. Laughton Road can be seen in the background. The Church is shown after it was extended.

LAUGHTON ROAD, DINNINGTON. Shows the Brightside and Carbrook Co-op to the right and the houses built for the managers of the colliery to the left.
The Technical School has still to be built and the trees in the far background mark Throapham.

LAUGHTON ROAD, DINNINGTON.

Frisby's shop is to the right looking up towards the Church. 1950s.

LAUGHTON ROAD, DINNINGTON. The bank nearly off photograph is still used as a bank. Next to this is a barbers shop with its pole on display. One of the shopkeepers stands outside in his snow white apron.

DINNINGTON HALL, off Nursery Road. The Home of the Athorpe Family who were falconers to the King. The Falcon Inn was named after them.

Dean's Restaurant Dinnington 1969 - 1977. This building was originally the Dean family home with a small shop in the front room which was entered directly from the front door.
It was the stopping place for many families and children before catching a bus.

VIEW FROM THE AIR OF LAUGHTON ROAD 1950. The white bus belongs to Fosters Garage, the owners of which lived down Swinston Hill Road (formally Worksop Lane). The group of buildings to the far left is one of the early farms. The second Manor House for Dinnington can be seen behind the garage, now demolished.

FALCON SQUARE, DINNINGTON. Wigmores bus waiting to the right and the Sheffield bus to the left. The marks of the extension to the church still show on the roof. The church wall can be seen behind Wigmores bus and the road behind is Laughton Road.

BARLEYCROFT LANE, DINNINGTON. 1908

Many of these buildings are still in existence today although they are greatly altered.

CONSTABLE LANE 1995. Although this photograph is modern the buildings to the rear are old farm buildings and the second graveyard is still in existence on this road.

EASTERN AVENUE, DINNINGTON, 1926. These were the second stage of purpose built colliery houses. Where the lamppost is there is a small cul de sac leading off with more housing. This photograph was probably taken soon after the houses were built.

DINNINGTON TERRACE 1905-1910. This terrace of housing was believed to be the first built for miners from the colliery and housed those still living in Tin Town.

BARLEYCROFT LANE, DINNINGTON. With its junction with Laughton Road and showing the still existent bank on the left. Further along on the left the building became the Barleycroft Public House. The first purpose built school is at the far end of this road on the left and is adjacent to the Middleton Institute.

LEOPOLD STREET, DINNINGTON 1920 - This cul-de-sac led towards Barleycroft Lane.
Note the old pram and the long dresses on the women.

Dinnington Miners Welfare 1966. The rocking horse is still there but the swings which used to be where the chairs are have gone.

Construction of Dinnington Colliery with one of the winding gears for the cages going down the pit.

Coal cart on Outgang Lane Dinnington.

Dinnington Main Colliery 1920. It had its own trucks for taking coal out and materials in.

PLANTATION AVENUE, DINNINGTON 1977. On the site of the old Tin Town. Note how close the pit tip was to these houses. An accident waiting to happen! These houses were a vast improvement for the miners when they were first built.

LAUGHTON ROAD, DINNINGTON. Date approximately turn of the 1900s. J.Whitakers shop and Stamp's bike shop.

Students from Dinnington Technical School 1935

LAUGHTON ROAD, DINNINGTON. At its junction with Barleycroft Lane, the wall outside the bank is long gone. At this time there were no houses to the left hand side.

Falcon View with the church in the background. The building to the left is a lodging house and was formerly the Workhouse where a suspected murder was committed.

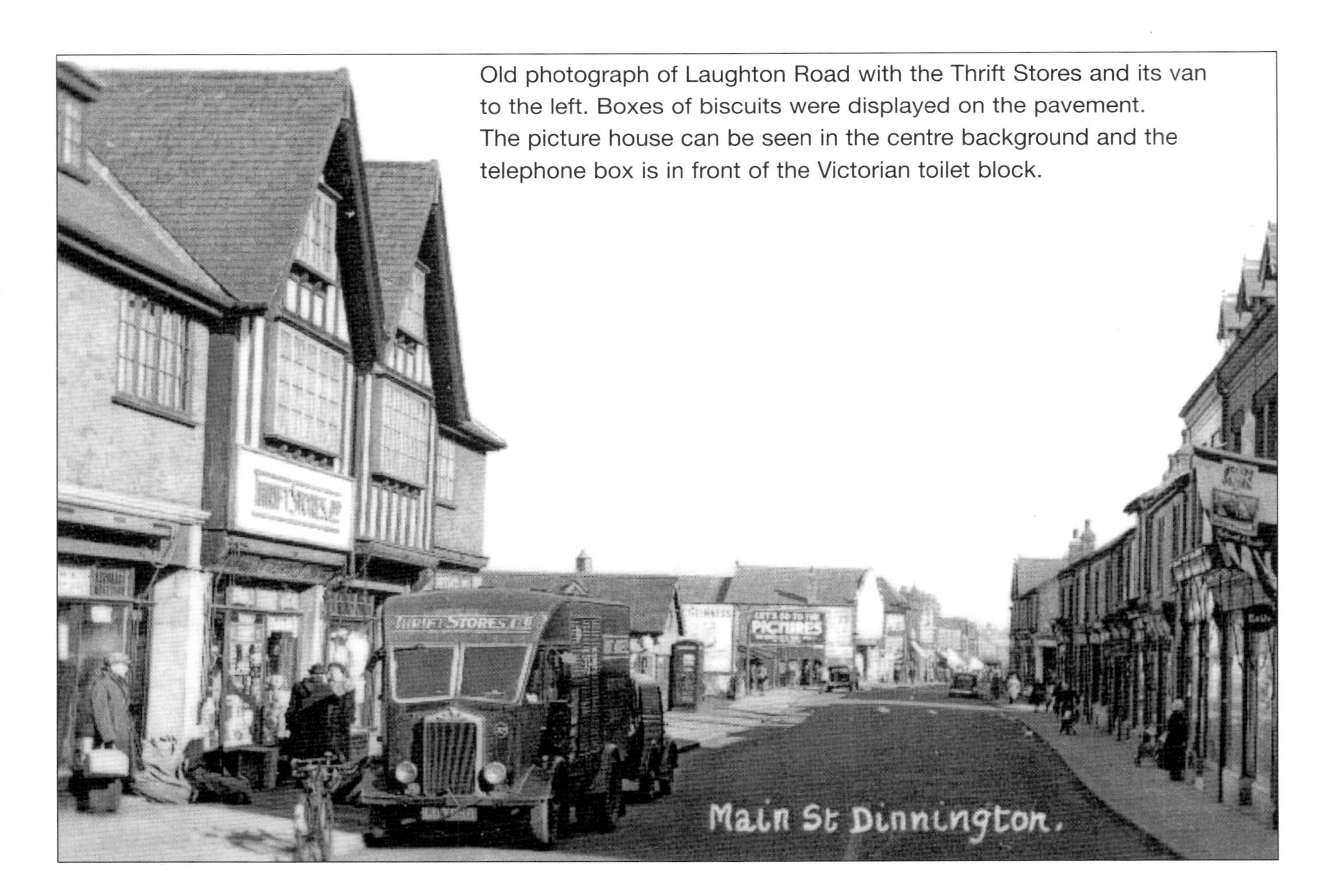

Old photograph of Laughton Road with the Thrift Stores and its van to the left. Boxes of biscuits were displayed on the pavement. The picture house can be seen in the centre background and the telephone box is in front of the Victorian toilet block.

Mr Brewer's House at the top of Laughton Road, Dinnington. These houses are opposite the church wall. The blacksmiths is in the background.

Top part of 'The Wapping' at Laughton. Marked on maps as the top of Workhouse Hill. The building jutting out into the road was the former workhouse.

Dinnington firemen in their shiny uniforms, approximately 1910. Note their proud faces.

Tin Town, Dinnington Colliery. This view is taken from the pit tip with coal trucks tipping coal waste in the foreground. Note how close the tip was to the miners homes. The miners lived in these tin huts with their families. People were born, lived and died in these close proximity conditions. The death rate was horrendous. These were the days of no running water or sanitation.

Cottages on Church Lane Dinnington.

The building to the left is still there. Note the worn down stone paving slabs to the left.

Falcon Square, Dinnington. To the left of the Old Falcon Inn is the old Pinfold. c1904

Dinnington Hall 1905. The James Paine drawing room can be seen jutting out to the left of the building behind the frontage.

St. Leonard's Church. This photograph is prior to any proper road surface. A bus shelter replaced the tree on the left.

The bottom of Laughton Road Dinnington looking up towards the church.

Kiveton Park c1957. The effects of the war can still be seen with brown paint on the outside of buildings.

Kiveton Park Colliery, date unknown. Many railway lines leading in and out. It had its own signal box on the right.

Railway crash at Kiveton Park c1905

Toll Bar at Kiveton Park with its house for the toll taker.

John Pardoe's shop on Doe Quarry Lane Dinnington.

Freda Turner next to her well in Laughton. The Turner family owned the building known as Ye Old Village Shop for over 350 years.

LORDENS HILL, DINNINGTON 1909. All the trees and hedges have gone and a housing estate is on the fields to the right.

Dinnington Station at Laughton common. Now only one line exists and all the station buildings have gone.

St. Leonard's Church before the roads had tarmac laid. Note the chimney on the roof of the side aisle.

Church Lane Dinnington looking down from the top. The buildings to the right are still there.
A very rare photograph.

A lovely view of laughton Vicarage at the early part of the last century.

Dinnington Carnival with a man dressed as an American Indian on a farm horse. Early 1900s.

SOUTH STREET, DINNINGTON. Some of the earliest Miners' houses in the village. These were built on the old site of 'Tin Town'.

SOUTH ANSTON. Taken in the entrance to the Church Yard. The sign shows the road to North Anston and then Dinnington. The Leeds Arms is in the far background, the road to the left leads to Kiveton.

An early photograph of Dinnington Colliery with the wooden cooling tower in the foreground.
This was Dinnington Colliery in its heyday.

Laughton Church of England village school built in the reign of Queen Elizabeth 1st.
Believed to be the oldest village school in Yorkshire. Note the early mullioned windows.

FIRBECK HALL. Once regular visited by the then Prince of Wales when it was one of the most luxurious country clubs in the country. Henry Hall often broadcast from here, Charlie Kunz the famous pianist was a regular performer there and Amy Johnson the record breaking pilot often stayed here. Firbeck had its own airfield and was used often by people staying at the country club.

OLD HALL FARM. The Home of the Wise Virgin in 1652. A fascinating time in the history of Laughton.

THE WISE
VIRGIN.
OR,
A wonderfull Narration of
the various Diſpenſations of God towards a Childe of eleven years of age; wherein as his ſeverity hath appeared in afflicting, ſo alſo his goodneſs both in enabling her (when ſtricken dumb, deaf and blinde, through the prevalency of her diſeaſe) at ſeveral times to utter many glorious Truths concerning *Chriſt*, *Faith*, and other ſubjects; and alſo in Recovering her without the uſe of any external means, leſt the glory ſhould be given to any other.
To the wonderment of many that came far and neer to ſee and hear her.
She is the daughter of Mr. *Anthony Hatfeild* Gentleman, in *Laughton* in *Yorkſhire*; her name is
MARTHA HATFEILD.

The works of the Lord are great, ſought out of all them that have pleaſure therein, Pſal.111.2.
All thy works ſhall praiſe thee, O Lord, and thy Saints ſhall bleſs thee, Pſal.145.10.
Natura in minimis maximè mirabilis.
The ſecond Edition enlarged, with ſome paſſages of her gracious converſation now in the time of health.
By *James Fiſher*, a Servant of CHRIST and Miniſter of the Goſpel in *Sheffeild*.

LONDON,
Printed for *John Rothwell*, at the Fountain and Bear in *Cheap-ſide*. MDCLIV.

The Wise Virgin
Laughton

In 1652 Martha, the twelve year old daughter of Anthony and Faith Hatfeild, gained national notoriety when she was seized by an illness which caused her to have fits that prevented her from moving or seeing. During these fits she was able to speak and astonished people with the piety and wisdom of her utterances. Visitors and pilgrims came from far and wide to see her. Between 1653 and 1664 a book about her, "The Wise Virgin", ran to five editions. After eight months the fits passed and normality returned to Laughton. The Hatfeild dynasty of Laughton lasted until 1791 when the unmarried John Hatfeild died.

The double hanging on the 10th of September 1864, was of murderers James Sargisson from Laughton and Joseph Myers from Sheffield. Myers had tried to cheat the hangman by cutting his throat while in prison but was saved by the surgeon. The hangings were reported in detail by The Leeds Mercury newspaper which claimed that between 80,000 to 100,000 people had come to watch the event on that Saturday morning. At five minutes to nine, the prison bell began to toll and inside the two men were being pinioned by Thomas Askern of York. They were led out onto the gallows supported on each side by warders and preceded by the Under Sheriff and the Chaplain. Askern pulled down the white caps over their faces but both men continued to speak, Sargisson's last words to Myers were reportedly "Art thou happy lad?" to which Myers responded 'Indeed I am." Askern then operated the drop which fell with a thud, their bodies being almost completely hidden from the crowd. Myers seemed to die almost immediately, but Sargisson struggled for some minutes. After hanging for the customary hour, they were removed from the gallows and buried within the prison.

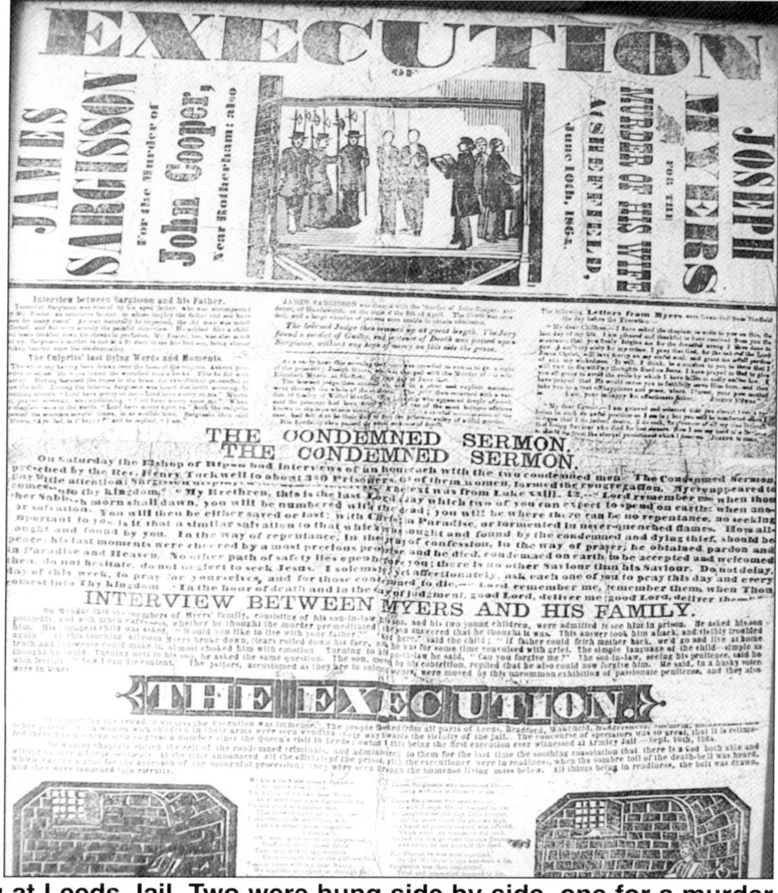

EXECUTION OF

JOSEPH MYERS FOR THE MURDER OF HIS WIFE AT SHEFFIELD, June 10th, 1864.

JAMES SARGISSON For the Murder of John Cooper, Near Rotherham: also

THE CONDEMNED SERMON.

INTERVIEW BETWEEN MYERS AND HIS FAMILY.

THE EXECUTION.

Notice telling of the public hanging at Leeds Jail. Two were hung side by side, one for a murder committed in Laughton, and one for a murder in Sheffield. This was the last public hanging at Leeds Jail.

A CHARABANC. Local residents of Dinnington setting off on a day trip to the seaside. Note the solid tyres.

DINNINGTON COLLIERY 1902

Dinnington Colliery being sunk. Note the wheel housing under construction and the power housing being built.

Cleaning out the grate of an old range which would be black leaded every week. The oven made lovely rice puddings, bread and baked potatoes.

This photo shows the conditions many miners worked under at Dinnington Colliery. This was the time of the pick and shovel and often the roof was lower than this.

Geo.Thickitt, Butchers, Laughton Road, Dinnington.

Mr Billam - The last Cordwainer, a maker and repairer of shoes. Laughton

August 1914, First World War enlistment photograph taken outside the Place Cinema, Dinnington. How many of these never came home?

New Street formally 'The Barracks', built at the early days of the sinking of Dinnington Colliery.

High St. Laughton. The St.Leger Arms is on the left. The gap between the two buildings is the entrance to the blacksmiths.

Dinnington Band. This band won numerous awards in the late 1950s.

Coronation Gardens Dinnington with the old bandstand. The building in the background to the right is the old Junior School.

The demolition of Falcon Square bus shelter 1960s..

Broughs grocery shop on Laughton Rd, Dinnington with all the staff outside (note the price of butter per pound).

The Thornton Family of Thurcroft who started
the first bus service from Laughton to Wickersley.
Note the solid tyres and the warning bell at the front.

Laughton Bible Class F.C 1920s

Dinnington Colliery Institute Cricket Team. 1st XI 1932.
Winners of the Bassetlaw League Championship and "Worksop Guardian" Cup.

B. Lidget. W. Mee. H. Hayes. C. Hargreaves. H. Flowers. H. Higham. P. King. C. Buxton (Scorer).
S. Downes. J. Higham. J.T. Atter (Captain). E. Dann. E. Atter.

St Leonard's Football Team 1922-23

Dinnington Athletic F.C First XI

A very early photograph of Falcon Square long before the church was extended and before cars, buses and pavements. The coal wagon has just tipped a load outside the cottage to the left.

Dinnington 'new' Schools c1913. The Junior School is to the left and the infants school to the right.

Falcon Square c1905. The tree in the centre was replaced by the bus shelter. The building to the right is a farmhouse, latterly Deans shop then restaurant.

Herbert Hirst a local personality, and his steam roller at New Road end in Dinnington. All machines at this time were powered by steam including farm machinery. They were never short of work.

The Miners Institute. This was a hive of activity, the bowling green is still there today.

A class at Dinnington Council Infant School. Note the class is all girls. Girls were taught separately and even had their own playgrounds.

Parents waiting for their children outside Dinnington Junior School c1936. Most children educated there say it was strict but fair and gave a good education. Photo taken on a hot day as most of the windows are open.

HIGH ST, LAUGHTON. The road behind the paraffin van leads off to Firbeck. The shop on the right belonged to the Dobbs family. They had a cycle shop downstairs and a dentist upstairs. What a wonderful view with no cars or fumes.

LORDENS HILL, DINNINGTON c1910. The children are posing for the photographer. Note the boy in his fancy clothes with the poorer children. A large housing estate for miners was later built on the fields to the right.

Wagons and bicycles on a local lane. The actual site is unknown but the photograph gives us a view of a typical country scene in an era long gone. c1910.

The Cross Roads at Kiveton Park pre 1918

Hard Lane. A different view of the same crossroads.

Kiveton Park c1930. Early pushchair and boy in short trousers on the pavement.

Kiveton Park c1957. There were very few cars on the road at this time because people could not afford them, only vicars, doctors and the wealthy drove them.

LAUGHTON ROAD, DINNINGTON. Barleycroft Lane is off to the right, the old farm buildings to the left are still in existence. The entrance to the manor house was via the gap in the wall behind the farm.

DINNINGTON MANOR HOUSE. This building should never have been demolished. The present Co-op building is now at this site.

Thompson's Bakers and Confectioners on Laughton Road. This was one of the shops where children used to press their faces up to the window longing for the delights displayed.

LAUGHTON ROAD, DINNINGTON. The Electric Theatre is now the Lyric Theatre. Dinnington as a village had all the shops it needed for its residents including the shoe shop shown on the left and the pawn brokers which was across the road.

Corner of Silverdales Road and Lordens Hill. 1910.
Whenever a photograph was going to be taken they tried to get members of the public to come out and pose.
Silverdales Road leads off to the right.

Laughton Road, Dinnington showing the early influx of shops to service the incoming miners.

Bawtry Road, Bramley 1902-1915. Early cottages built for agricultural workers in the village.

Throapham Manor House which was later used as an overspill for the Technical College. Another historical manor house that should never have been demolished.

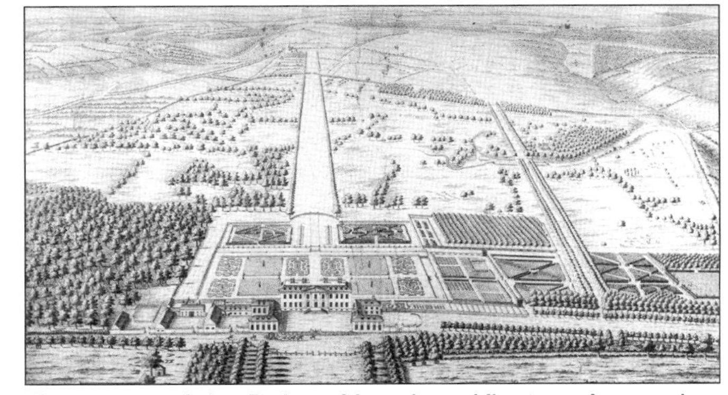

The estate of the Duke of Leeds at Kiveton. As can be seen this was an extensive estate and also included the surrounding villages

A lovely photograph showing the second Falcon Inn in its heyday. It shows the tudor style building when it was first built. In the distance can be seen the lodging house, formally the workhouse. In the centre is the horse trough dedicated to Mr Gurnal. It can now be seen in Coronation Park on Laughton Road.

Old Toll Bar House, Todwick.

Old Hall, Kiveton Lane, Todwick c1960.

Inside Todwick Church c1944. Note the early round arch to the chancel and the box pews.

Old Shepherd's Cottages, Todwick.

St Leger Arms in Laughton. Named after the landowner of that name at the turn of the last century. It is now extended and modernised but traces of the old building can still be seen.

St Peters Church, Thorpe Salvin.

Thorpe Salvin 1950s.

Thorpe Salvin 1905.

Thorpe Salvin derelict Hall in the background. The early gatehouse is still in existence in front of the building but cannot be seen in this photograph. The wall to the left is the church wall.

High St, Laughton around 1890.
All the children were wearing their best clothes for Whit Sunday.
The small wall to the left is all that remains of the Golden Ball public house.

The Guest family working at Laughton Village Smithy. Mr Guest on the left was the last village blacksmith. The horse shoes were made on site. He made gates, hinges, rims for wheels and would also mend items for local villagers when needed. A true craftsman.

Doorway of All Saints Church, Laughton
Photograph of church doorway approx 1900.
The doorway is nationally famous for its Saxon origin using Roman stone.

CHURCH CORNER, LAUGHTON. The building to the right was where people used to go to collect disinfectant for their earth closets. Stone pillars mark the entrance to the early vicarage.

Firbeck Village largely unchanged to present time.

Barrel rolling competition near the old pit tip. Taken in the car park of the Squirrel Public House.

The Earl of Scarborough visiting the renovation work being carried out at Roche Abbey 1928.

Barker Hades Road, Letwell. A sleepy hamlet much the same today c1905.

Bottom part of 'The Wapping' Laughton. The road to the right is High Street. The buildings on the right were 'one up and one down' houses, - demolished for road widening. The village pump on the right has also gone. Where the children are standing is the entrance to the blacksmiths, they used to love to watch the blacksmith working. A lovely education.

LAUGHTON ROAD, DINNINGTON c1907. Looking up towards the church. Living accommodation was above the shops. Just before Christmas most shops held a treasure trove for the children.

LAUGHTON ROAD, DINNINGTON. An early motor cycle and sidecar is in the foreground. Many families bought this form of transport before they could afford a motor car. These were the days when Dinnington was alive and many families owned shops. c1920

Stable block for Dinnington Hall, the home of the Athorpes. These buildings are still in existence including the wall with the original pillars.

Early aerial view of Falcon Square with Church Lane and the fields surrounding the area still in existence. The bus shelter is in the centre of the square. The old Manor House which has long been a farm house can be seen by its roof in the foreground. Many of the buildings have long gone including the boarding house which was originally the Workhouse to the rear of the church.